WHO BUILT THAT?

WHO BUILT THAT?
MODERN HOUSES

An Introduction to Modern Houses and Their Architects

Didier Cornille

Princeton Architectural Press · New York

INTRODUCTION

Architecture may seem complex and difficult to understand, but it's also quite fascinating. This book teaches you, as simply as possible, about a variety of houses designed by great modern architects.

The pages that follow invite you to visit these houses and discover how they were built. You'll learn how each architect invented a new way of creating buildings.

Modern architecture will no longer feel so mysterious, and perhaps you, too, will dream of designing a house one day.

CONTENTS

1924 THE SCHRÖDER HOUSE

GERRIT RIETVELD

EVERYTHING IS MOVEABLE

Built in 1924 by the architect Gerrit Rietveld in Utrecht, the Netherlands, this is the oldest of the modern houses in this book.

Born in 1888, Gerrit Rietveld studied architecture before becoming a cabinetmaker. During this time he created an unusual chair made of simple planks of painted wood, called the Red and Blue Chair (1918).

His work was inspired by the artists of the de Stijl movement, who created abstract paintings composed only of lines and rectangular shapes in primary colors: blue, red, and yellow. Their master was Piet Mondrian, a Dutch painter.

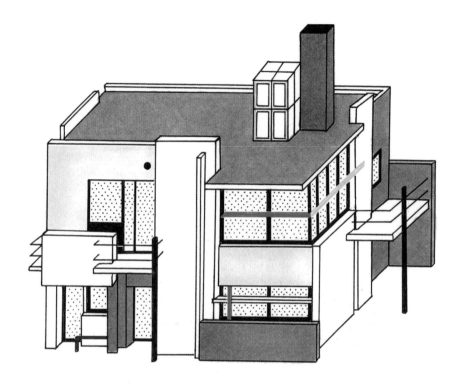

The newly widowed Mrs. Schröder wanted to begin a new life with her children, a boy and two girls. Passionate about avant-garde (new and experimental) architecture, she wanted a light-filled house without inside walls. If you look closely at this small building (thirty-three feet or ten meters wide), you will realize that its outside walls seem independent from one another, as if they were floating in air.

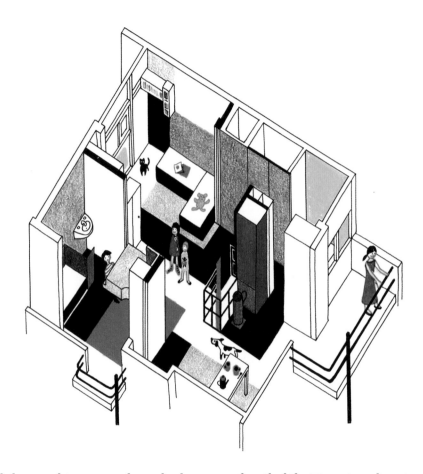

Mrs. Schröder worked with her architect to adapt the house to family life. To enjoy the view, she and her children spent most of their time on the second floor, which contains one large room bathed in light.

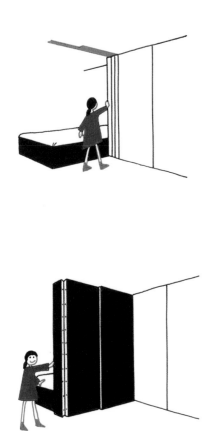

At night they could use a system of sliding panels to create separate rooms.

1931 VILLA SAVOYE

LE CORBUSIER

A TRULY MODERN HOME

Born in Switzerland, Charles-Édouard Jeanneret (1887–1965) took the name Le Corbusier in 1920, when he started his career as a painter and urban architect. He worked for some time as a draftsman for the Perret Brothers, the pioneers of reinforced concrete,[*] in Paris, France.

* Concrete containing strengthening materials such as metal bars

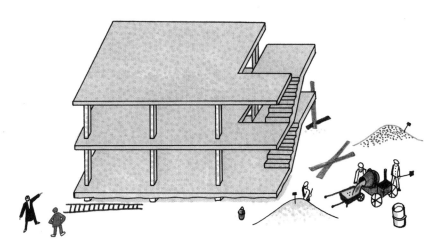

During World War I (1914–18), Le Corbusier invented a way of building with reinforced concrete that he called Dom-ino.

This building technique was based on units made of slabs supported by simple concrete posts. Like actual dominoes, Le Corbusier's Dom-inoes could be combined in many different ways.

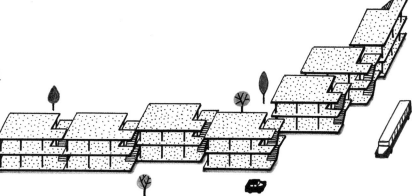

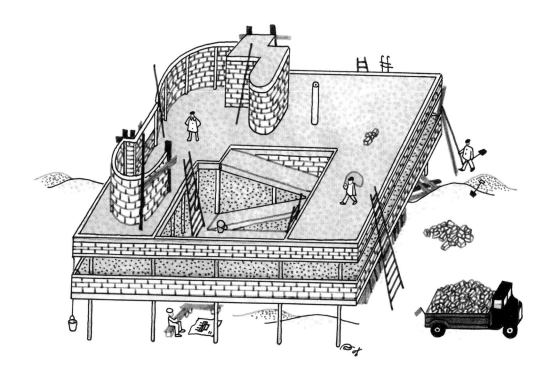

From 1928 to 1931, the architect constructed the Villa Savoye, a 1,340-square-foot (twenty meters on each side), two-story house in Poissy, France, near Paris.

This building represented his five rules for truly modern architecture:

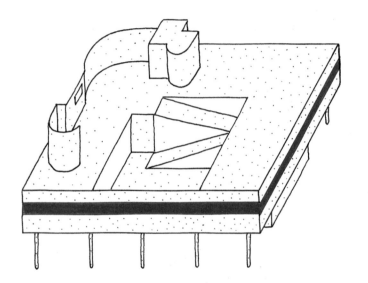

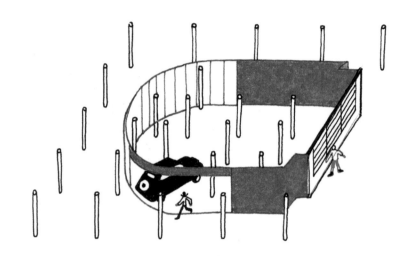

1) Stilts support the house so that, in Le Corbusier's words, "the house is a box in the air."

2) Open plan: the interior has no supporting walls, only partitions.* Here, they are rounded to guide cars toward the garage.

* Light walls used to divide space into rooms rather than to hold a building's weight

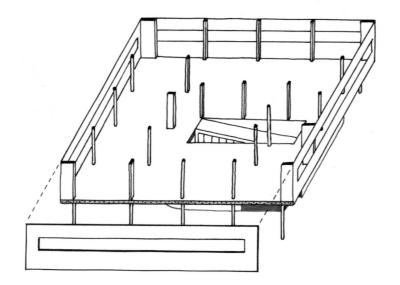

3) Free design of the facade:[*] the outside walls are simple, light, and thin.

* One of the sides of a building (usually its front)

4) Large, horizontal windows open all around onto the beautiful countryside.

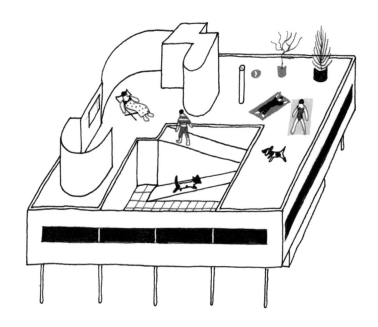

5) The flat roof is used as a garden, where people can enjoy the sun. It is almost like being on the deck of a cruise ship.

Le Corbusier also built:

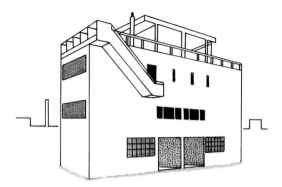

The Frugès Modern District, a housing development in Pessac, France (1925)

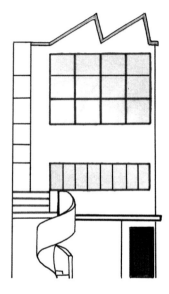

A house for the painter Amédée Ozenfant in Paris (designed with his brother, Pierre Jeanneret, 1922)

The Pavilion of the New Spirit in Paris (1924)

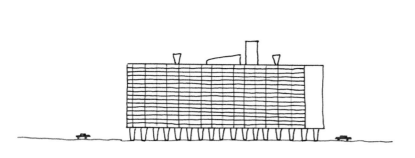

The Radiant City in Marseille, France (1952)

The Chapel of Notre-Dame-du-Haut in Ronchamp, France (1955)

The House of Man in Zurich, Switzerland (1963–67)

His own cottage in Roquebrune-Cap-Martin, France (1949), where he loved to relax

1939 **FALLINGWATER**

FRANK LLOYD WRIGHT

A HOUSE IN THE WILDERNESS

Frank Lloyd Wright was born in 1867 in Wisconsin.
As a child, he spent his vacations on his uncle's farm
and discovered the beauty of the American countryside,
inspiring his love of nature.

As an architect, he created houses that were adapted to the climates and landscapes of the United States.

The sprawling Frederick C. Robie House in Chicago, Illinois (1910), for example, has large roofs that provide shade and help keep the building cool.

The Laura R. Gale House in Oak Park, Illinois (1909), is surrounded by large balconies, so that the view can be admired from all sides.

The owners of this house, Edgar and Liliane Kaufmann, had a large store in Pittsburgh, Pennsylvania. Their son worked in Wright's studio for some time, during which the Kaufmanns met the architect and asked him to design a weekend house for them—the famous Fallingwater.

Mr. and Mrs. Kaufmann wanted their house to be
located in an extraordinary place, nestled in the forest
in front of a beautiful waterfall. Wright preferred
to build the house directly on top of the water, so the
couple would live surrounded by this spectacle
of nature.

Wright built massive stone walls on the rocky terrain
and hung large reinforced-concrete balconies above
the waterfall.

The inside is like a furnished cave: a fire crackles in the living room, where a boulder peeks through the stone floor. It's a house for relaxing, far from the city—all is well here.

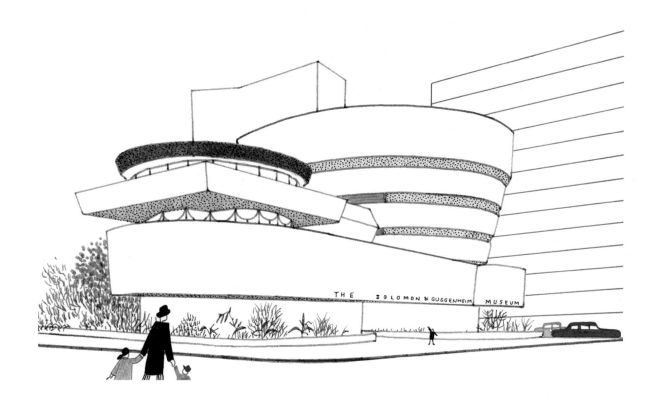

Wright later designed many more houses, as well as the Solomon R. Guggenheim Museum in New York City (1959).

1949 THE EAMES HOUSE

CHARLES & RAY EAMES

MULTICOLORED AND FULL OF INVENTIONS

This pair of American designers wanted to bring comfort to people all over the world. During World War II (1939–45), they used industrial machinery to make plywood splints and stretchers for the injured.

After the war, using what they learned from their experience in industrial manufacturing, the Eameses explored new materials and designed many unique pieces of furniture, such as this strange fiberglass chair called La Chaise (1948)…

…and this really comfortable chair known as the Lounge Chair (1956).

They also invented toys for their grandchildren:

The Elephant (1945)

The House of Cards (1952)

In 1945 they launched a project to build houses out of standard materials. Their own home, located in the Pacific Palisades near Los Angeles, California, would serve as the model.

The Eames House was designed like a simple warehouse, sixty feet long by twenty feet wide (eighteen by six meters), and was built like a steel Erector set. From afar it looks like the skeleton of a giant mammoth.

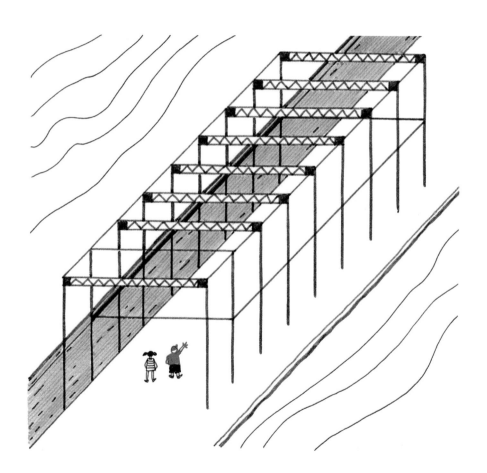

But the final house is not as plain as you might think: the designers added different-colored panels as well as windows that open in all directions, creating a very cheerful home.

From the outside the building blends with the landscape.

The inside is a marvelous universe, filled with plants and objects from all over the world.

1951 THE FARNSWORTH HOUSE

MIES VAN DER ROHE

A MINIMALIST* HOUSE

Originally from Germany, Ludwig Mies van der Rohe (1886–1969) was first and foremost a mason and thus had a thorough knowledge of construction materials. He later became an architect and was the last director of the great school of design called the Bauhaus, in Germany.

* Simple and undecorated

Mies moved to the United States just before World War II and designed beautiful houses and buildings there. His favorite materials were metal and glass, which allowed him to be bold in his creations.

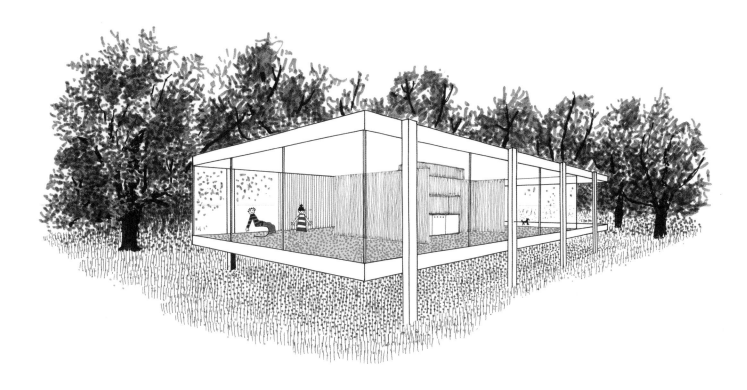

This is the Farnsworth House, near Chicago in Plano, Illinois.

Because the site* tends to flood,
the house had to be raised, like a bridge,
and is supported by eight steel posts.

* The place where a building is located

The building is rectangular, measuring
108 feet long and 40 feet wide (33 by
12 meters), with a small terrace in front.
The white color of the steel frame and the
large areas of glass make it stand apart
from the natural surroundings while
remaining unobtrusive.

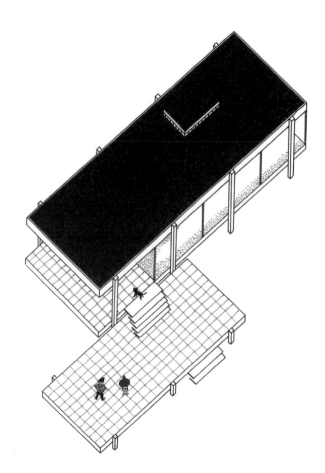

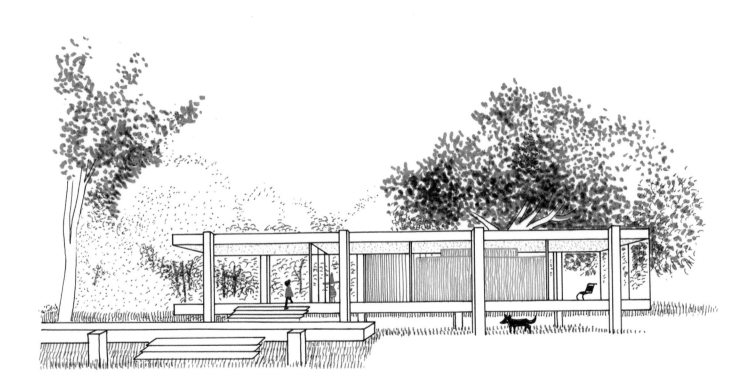

Inside the house there are only a few partitions, which create different zones. This makes it possible to move around freely and enjoy the scenery outside, although large curtains can be drawn for privacy.

Mies is famous for his numerous glass-and-steel structures. His designs, such as the Seagram Building in New York City (1958), are very clean and have a bold elegance.

1956 THE HOUSE FOR BETTER DAYS

JEAN PROUVÉ

A HOME FOR EVERYONE

Born in 1901 in Nancy, France, Jean Prouvé was the son of artists. He began his career as a blacksmith, discovering the possibilities of metal. He was especially interested in folded sheet metal, a lightweight and solid material.

Standard Chair (1934)

Compass Table (1950)

In his workshop, he designed and produced school furniture—and even houses—out of sheet metal.

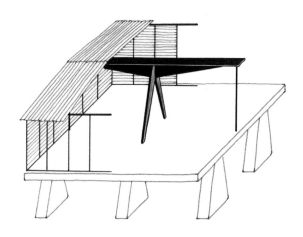

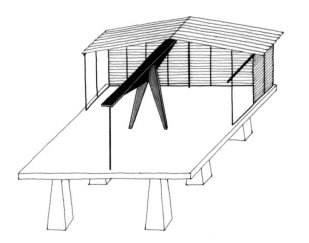

Portico Houses (1945)
Maxéville Factory

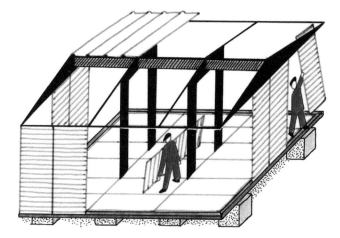

The various elements for these buildings were
eventually prefabricated (premade) in the factory,
then assembled on the construction site.

The winter of 1954 was terrible in France, so the Catholic priest Abbé Pierre appealed to the French people for help in housing the homeless. He reached out to Prouvé and asked him to design a prefabricated house that would be affordable for everyone.

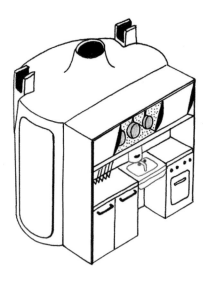

The result was a house with a block of metal in its center that contains the kitchen and the bathroom. This unit also supports the roof of the house.

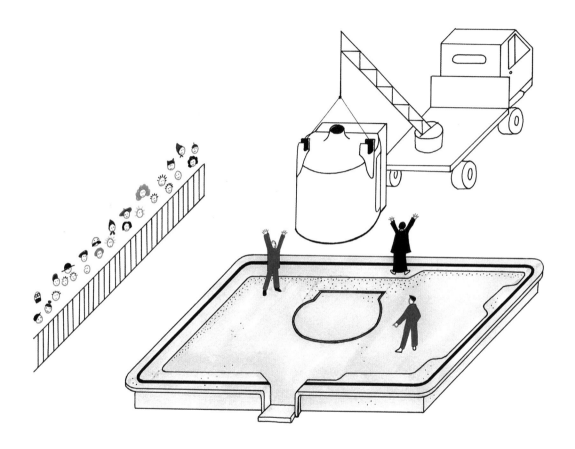

The assembly of the prototype (model) took place publicly in Paris with the help of only two workers. After the approximately twenty-eight-by-twenty-two-foot (8.5-by-6.7-meter) concrete foundation was poured, the metal unit was brought in and placed in its middle.

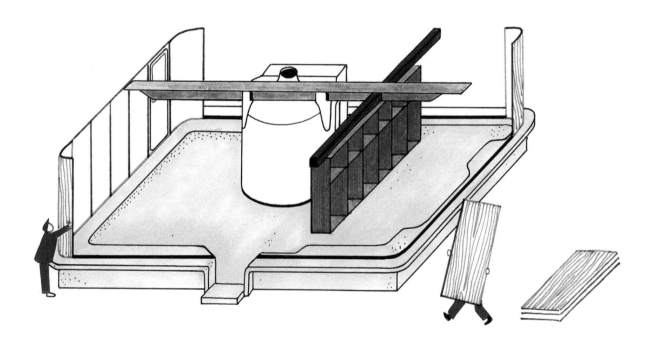

A steel girder* was added on top of the metal block, followed by dividing walls and, finally, the roof.

* A horizontal beam that supports a building

The home was built in only two days and could house a family with two children. Unfortunately, it was never mass-produced.

1978 GEHRY RESIDENCE

FRANK GEHRY

SMALL BECOMES LARGE

Frank Gehry was born in 1929. The Canadian architect traveled widely around Europe, where he met and was inspired by many artists. Like them, he loved to express himself very freely.

In 1977 Gehry bought a wooden house in Santa Monica, a Los Angeles suburb. The forty-by-thirty-two-foot (twelve-by-ten-meter) residence quickly became too small for his family, but he decided to keep and enlarge it. He surrounded it with a new wall, thus gaining space to install a new kitchen and dining room, using common materials, such as corrugated (wavy) sheet metal, plywood, and mesh.

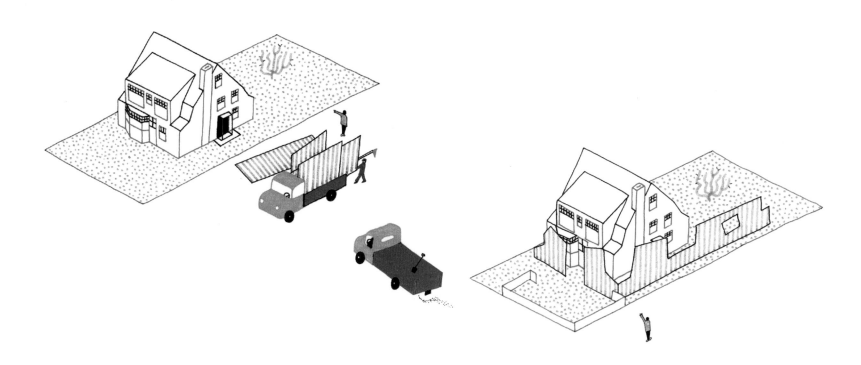

Then, he imagined that large glass cubes had fallen on the house and remained there in an unstable balance.

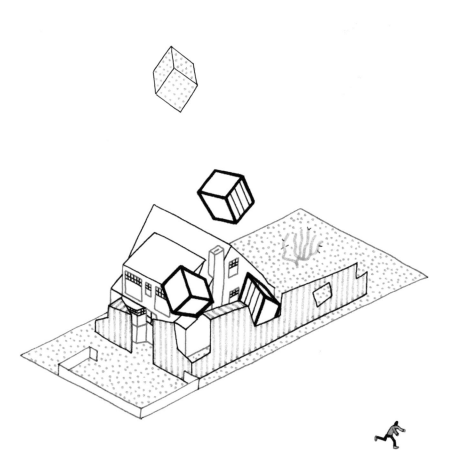

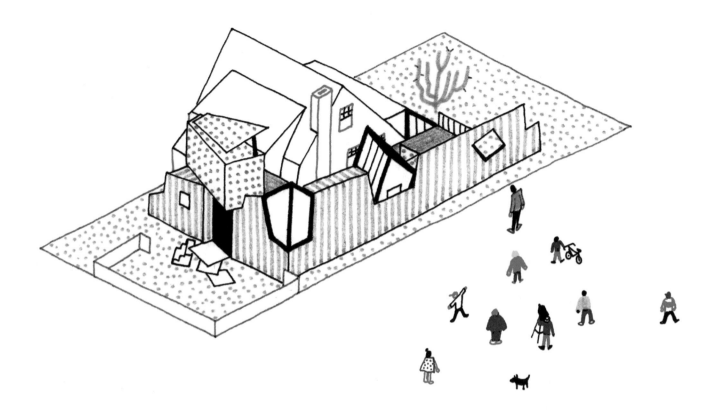

Two of these let light into the ground floor, and a third is used as an upstairs bedroom. The space inside the house was thus doubled. The building looks "deconstructed"—as if it had been taken apart and put back together—and attracts many curious onlookers.

Vitra Design Museum in Weil am Rhein,
Germany (1989)

The Dancing House in
Prague, Czech Republic
(1996)

Frank Gehry later built the Guggenheim Museum Bilbao in Spain (1997) and many other buildings
with surprising shapes.

1995 THE CARDBOARD HOUSE

SHIGERU BAN

AN ORDINARY MATERIAL USED IN AN EXTRAORDINARY WAY

Traditional Japanese houses are made of wood, with paper windows. They can easily be reconstructed after an earthquake, which occurs commonly in Japan. After the 1995 earthquake in Kobe, architect Shigeru Ban, born in 1957 in Tokyo, developed a house made of cardboard, a lightweight and widely available material, in order to rehouse the victims of the disaster.

Primarily built of cardboard rolls and other salvaged materials, the house can be built by volunteers.
Its shape can be square or rectangular.

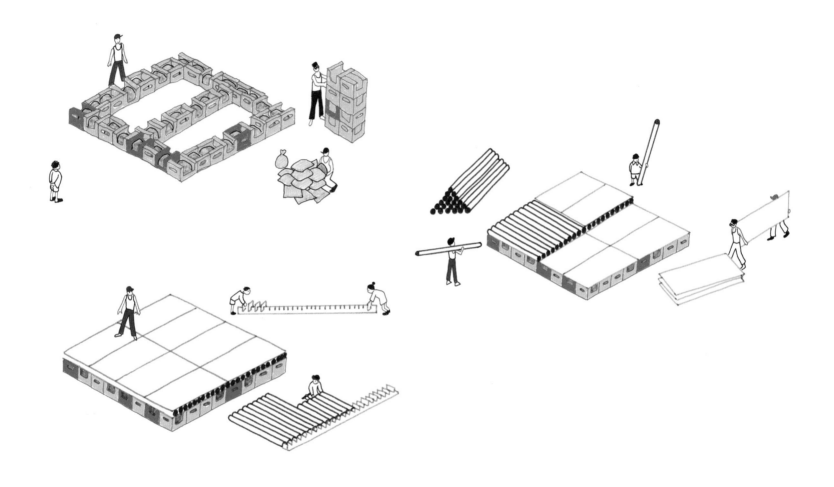

Plastic beer cases full of sandbags are laid down for the foundation.

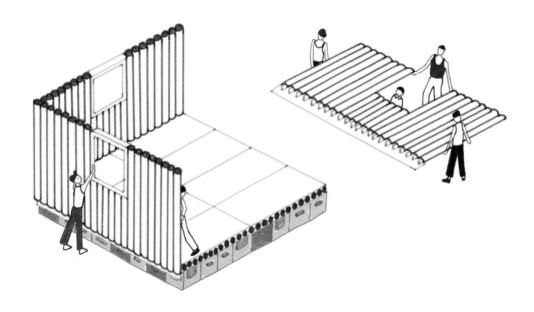

Next, cardboard tubes are arranged to make walls.

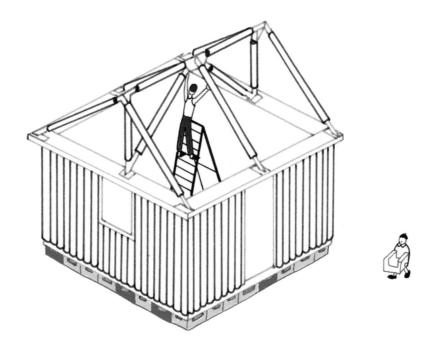

Then, a cardboard frame is added and covered with a plastic canvas.

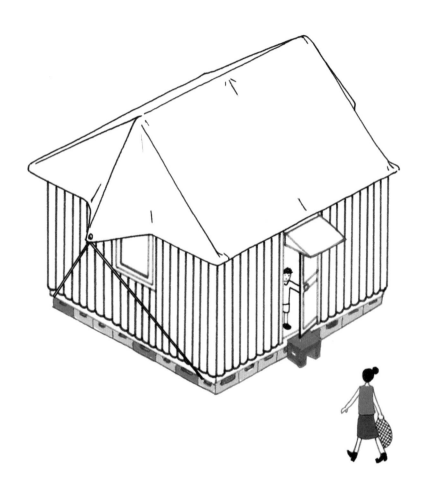

The house is finished!

Shigeru Ban designed many other cardboard houses, as well as wooden ones. In his hands ordinary materials become extraordinary.

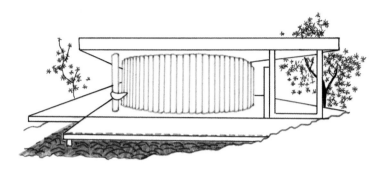

Paper Log House,
Yamanashi, Japan (1995)

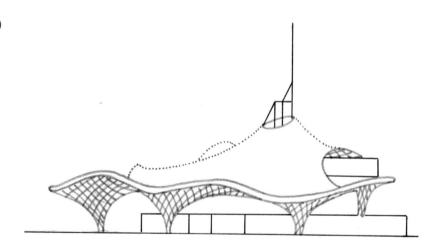

Pompidou Center, Metz, France, designed together
with Jean de Gastines (2010)

1998 THE BORDEAUX HOUSE

REM KOOLHAAS

AN ELEVATOR AS THE MAIN ROOM

Rem Koolhaas is a Dutch urbanist and architect. As an urbanist, he studied large cities such as Hanoi, Vietnam; Seoul, South Korea; and Shanghai, China, in Asia; Lagos, Nigeria, in Africa; and Houston, Texas, in the United States. In France, he drew up the map for Euralille, Lille's future business district.

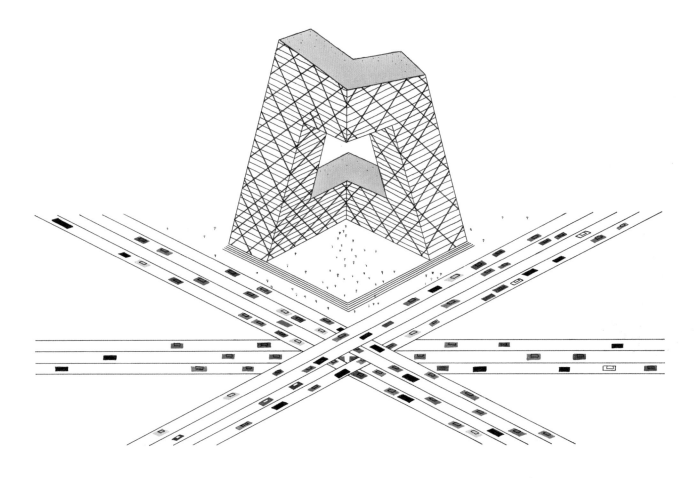

As an architect, he designed immense and surprising buildings, such as the headquarters for China Central Television in Beijing, China (2012).

This large, modern house, which he built not far from Bordeaux, France, is located in a park. The owner of this residence had been left paralyzed after a car accident, and the plan of the house takes his handicap into consideration.

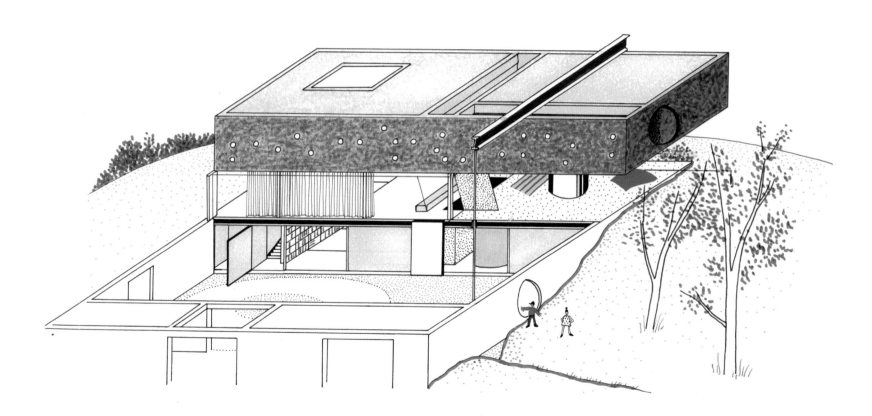

The most important space of the house is an elevator. In addition to providing access to all the floors, it also functions as an office. It's very large, measuring more than ten feet (three meters) on each side.

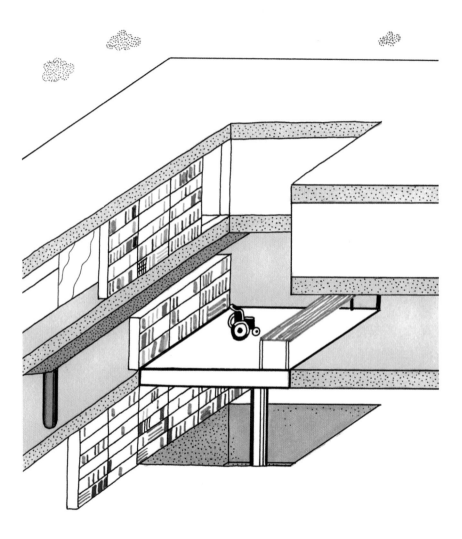

Each level of the house is different.

The basement feels like a cave, with a dark television room and a wine cellar.

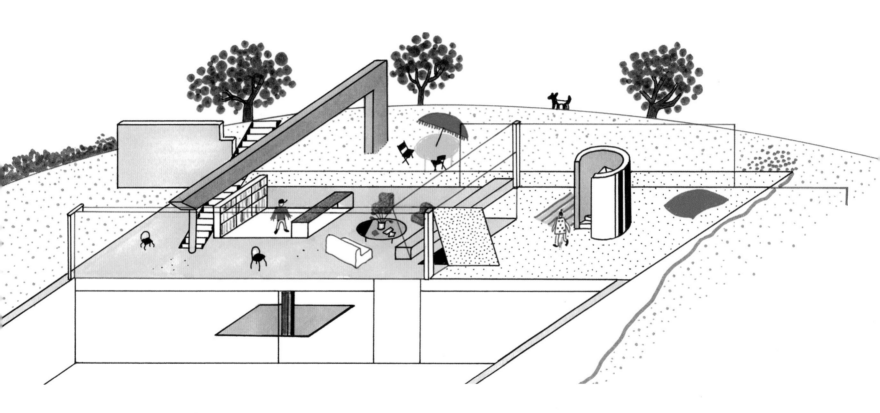

The ground floor is made of transparent glass.

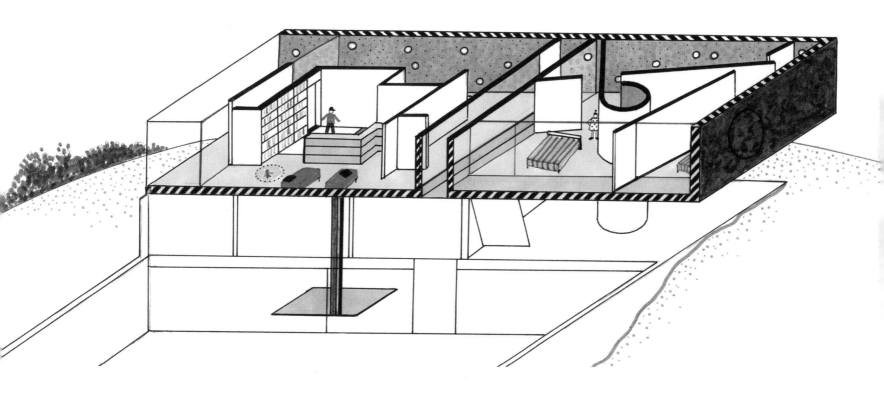

The bedroom walls on the second floor are dotted with portholes and form a large concrete box that opens to the sky in certain places.

2002 THE STRAW HOUSE

SARAH WIGGLESWORTH & JEREMY TILL

A GREEN HOUSE

These architects built their combined house and studio/office in the north of London over the course of four years. They designed everything with an eye to living in harmony with the environment. They have a vegetable garden and even a henhouse.

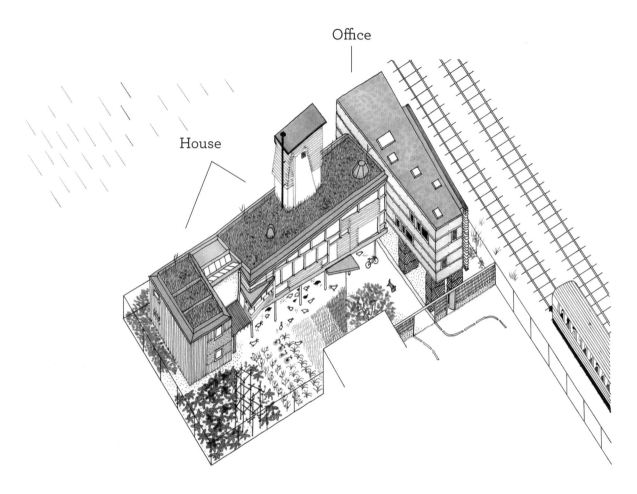

Office

House

From afar, the large house looks like a farm. The building containing the office helps block the noise of the nearby railway.

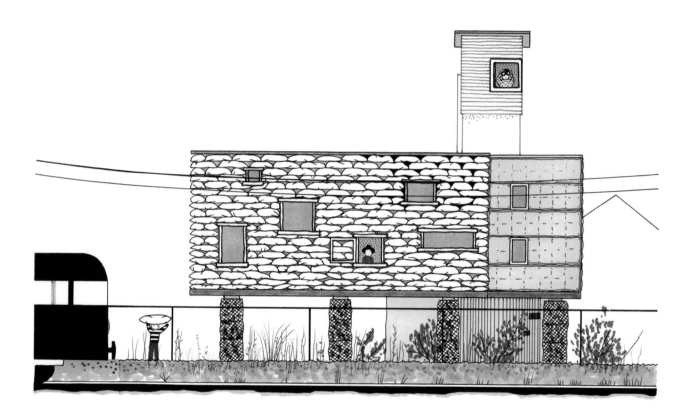

The office sits on stilts made out of recycled concrete. The side of the building that faces the railway is covered with a thick fabric that resembles a quilt, with sandbags stacked on top to soak up noise.

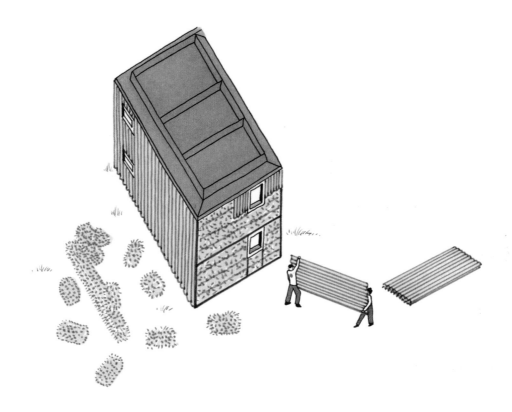

The walls of the house are made of straw, protected by sheet metal.

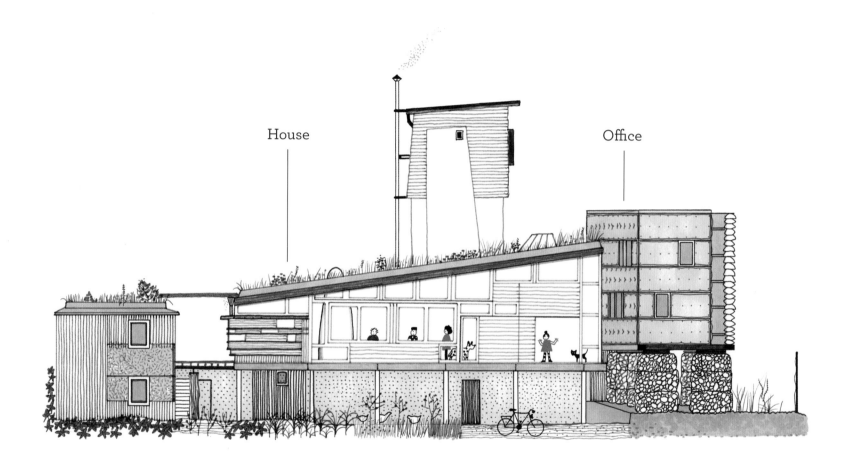

House

Office

The central part of the building is made of wood, with large windows that let in lots of light.
Food is stored in a cool pantry instead of a refrigerator.

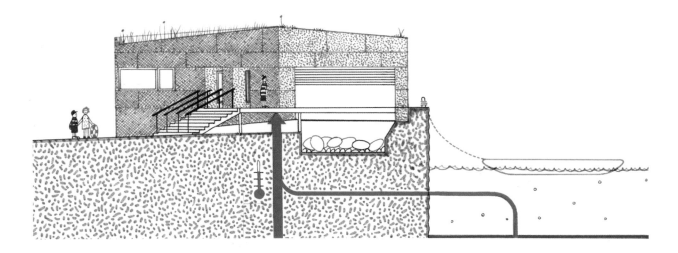

The Cremorne Riverside Centre, a canoeing center in London (2008)

Beyond this experiment in London, the architects have designed other durable and nature-friendly buildings.

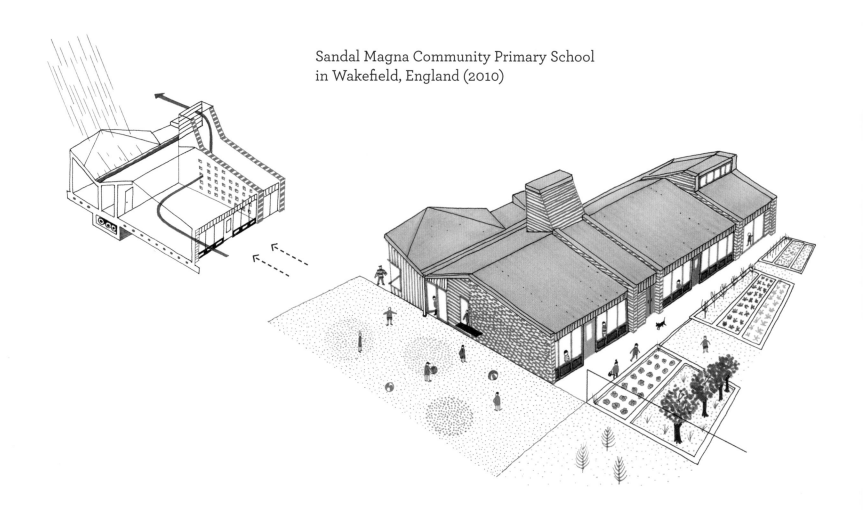

Sandal Magna Community Primary School
in Wakefield, England (2010)

Published in 2014 by
Princeton Architectural Press
A McEvoy Group Company
202 Warren Street
Hudson, New York 12534

Visit our website at www.papress.com.

First published in France under the title
Toutes les maisons sont dans la nature © 2012,
hélium/Actes Sud, Paris, France

Copyright English edition © 2014
Princeton Architectural Press

For Princeton Architectural Press:
Project editor: Nicola Brower
Typesetting: Paul Wagner

Special thanks to: Meredith Baber, Sara Bader,
Janet Behning, Megan Carey, Carina Cha,
Andrea Chlad, Barbara Darko, Benjamin English,
Russell Fernandez, Will Foster, Jan Hartman,
Jan Haux, Diane Levinson, Jennifer Lippert,
Katharine Myers, Jaime Nelson, Jay Sacher,
Rob Shaeffer, Sara Stemen, Marielle Suba, and
Joseph Weston of Princeton Architectural Press
—Kevin C. Lippert, publisher

Credits:

The Schröder House—Gerrit Rietveld
The drawings presented in the chapter dedicated to
Gerrit Rietveld are inspired by the artist's works,
© ADAGP, Paris, 2014.

Villa Savoye—Le Corbusier
The drawings presented in the chapter dedicated to Le
Corbusier are inspired by the artist's works, © F. L. C. /
© ADAGP, Paris, 2014.

Fallingwater—Frank Lloyd Wright
The drawings presented in the chapter dedicated to
Frank Lloyd Wright are inspired by the artist's works,
© ADAGP, Paris, 2014.

The Eames House—Charles & Ray Eames
The Eames House and the couple's designs appear by
courtesy of The Eames Foundation and Eames Office,
LLC. All copyright, trademark, trade dress, and all
other intellectual property and other rights reserved
(eamesoffice.com).

The Farnsworth House—Mies van der Rohe
The drawings presented in the chapter dedicated
to Mies van der Rohe are inspired by the artist's
works, © ADAGP, Paris, 2014.

The House for Better Days—Jean Prouvé
The drawings presented in the chapter dedicated
to Jean Prouvé are inspired by the artist's works,
© ADAGP, Paris, 2014.

Gehry Residence—Frank Gehry
© Frank O. Gehry. All rights reserved.

The Cardboard House—Shigeru Ban
© Shigeru Ban Architects

The Bordeaux House—Rem Koolhaas
The drawings presented in the chapter dedicated
to Rem Koolhaas are inspired by the artist's works,
© ADAGP, Paris, 2014.

**The Straw House—Sarah Wigglesworth &
Jeremy Till**
By courtesy of Sarah Wigglesworth & Jeremy Till.

Library of Congress
Cataloging-in-Publication Data
Cornille, Didier, 1951–
  [Toutes les maisons sont dans la nature. English]
  Modern houses : who built that? : an introduction to
modern houses and their architects / Didier Cornille.
  — First edition.
    83 pages : illustrations, (color) ; 18 x 26 cm.
  «First published in France under the title *Toutes les
maisons sont dans la nature* © 2012, Hélium, Paris,
France.»
    ISBN 978-1-61689-263-0 (alk. paper)
  1. Architect-designed houses—History—
20th centur—Juvenile literature. 2. Architect-designed
houses—History—century—Juvenile literature.
  I. Cornille, Didier, 1951- Toutes les maisons sont dans
la nature. Translation of: II. Title.
  NA7125.C3713 2014
  728—dc23
                                                    2014004391